Angie

Miri

Welcome to ¡Hola, Ola!

Your illustrated guide to the Spanish surf lingo.

Maybe you are about to go on the surf trip of your lifetime to the Spanish Northwest coast, or you are running away from the European winter to hit the Canary Islands. Whatever your surf destination, some basic Spanish surf lingo will make it much easier for you.

But learning a new language can be a challenge and let's be honest, the older we get, the harder it is to feed our brain with new stuff. During high school days, everything seemed pretty painless and learning a new language came kind of natural to us, but who really wants to go back to conjugating irregular verbs just to be able to communicate in the water?

We figured there had to be an easier way to get some Spanish into our heads. And here we go: ¡Hola, ola! Through illustrations and little anecdotes, we make it easy for you to remember all those essential words to survive in a Spanish surf environment. The German language has a great word for this kind of learning; an Eselsbrücke (aka donkey bridge), or mnemonic in English.

Funny fact: the little stories told in this book did actually happen. They are memories of the surf trips we have shared and surf stories we have experienced. We? That's us: Angie & Miri, and a whole group of passionate surfers and ocean lovers: the Epic Waves Family.

We hope you enjoy tagging along on our surf trip journeys and dedicate a wave to us when you confidently cruise through a Spanish speaking line-up.

Buenas olas,

Angie & Miri

Bombette

Rainbow

Ramonski

Lindis

Ray

Joshiño

Paul

Emilio Slater

Good old Lee

Melly

A surfear | gone surfing

Equipo de surf | surf equipment

Competencias sociales | social skills

Mundo surfero | surfers world

A surfear

- gone surfing -

Olas, basically means energy and moving water. And while some prefer the moving water to be tube shaped, others might prefer a more mellow type of energy. However, beggars can't be choosers and sometimes you take what you get.

So here they were in Tenerife. Their local surf guide Emilio Slater had taken them to an uncrowded town beach. A small bay beautifully nestled between rocks, palm trees and houses, but looking at the ocean Angie felt confused. There was massive swell hitting the bay, it was January after all, but the breaking **olas** were sort of mellow and reforming before hitting the beach. To be honest, she didn't really think how this could be fun to surf, but knowing Emilio, she trusted him to have a plan. And he certainly did.

Emilio explained that the local government had thrown massive rocks into the bay, to protect the sand to be washed away by the big winter swells. The rocks made the **olas** break before hitting the sandbank. The whitewash then passed the rocks and rolled into the bay, making it a perfect take-off zone for learning surfers. They then finished with a pretty fun shore break section.

But Angie didn't know all of this yet, when she was staring at the wave and saying to herself: hola **ola**, nice to meet you.

La ola (noun, feminine)

oh - lah (IPA: o-la)

wave

The object of our desire. Hollow, mushy, fat it doesn't matter. We simply love olas, in any shape and form.

Let's face it. As cool as it looks, surfing is not all sunshine. Realistically we are playing in a massive body of water and being moved around by sheer energy. The smooth rides we see in the videos are only a small part of what is going on out there.

So here she was, paddling for what seemed to be the biggest wave of the day. Her surf coach next to her was excitedly screaming: go for it, remember, commitment! Miri didn't want to disappoint her coach, so took a couple of deep strokes, felt the wave lifting her board and popped up. What followed was a hell of a ride down the wave´s face. Pure adrenaline.

Her scream of joy was only stopped by the sudden realization that her good old friend gravity had shown up, and she ended up straight in the flats. When the whitewash behind her hit, Miri prepared for the **lavadora**. Getting tossed around underwater, she curled up and let the ocean unload its energy. Few times in her life had she felt more alive than in this moment.

Exhausted but happy, Miri resurfaced, took a big breath and smiled. Smooth rides are great but still, surfing would only be half the fun without a proper **lavadora**.

La lavadora (noun, feminine)

lah-vah-doh-ra (IPA: la-βa-ðo-ɾa)

washing machine

The moment after a wipe-out when you are submerged and get tossed around by the ocean. Classic love-hate relationship.

Where you find breaking waves hitting the shore, you find water moving back into the ocean. Not exactly rocket science, but often overlooked or simply ignored. These **corrientes**, or channels, sometimes hide, but as long as waves are breaking, they are there. Promised!

Not that they didn't know and as experienced surfers, Bombette and Ray were able to identify the waters' flow. But being engaged in a delighted conversation about life, they simply didn't care and slowly drifted off further out to sea.

Sure, checking their reference points would have helped them to stay in position. But then again, they were too busy exchanging the secrets of life. Meanwhile, surf coaches Joshiño and Ramonski were watching from a distance and wondering about how much those ladies could actually talk. Would they ever stop?? Or would the **corriente** take them all the way to Jamaica?

Eventually, they too realized how far they had drifted out. The beach, which had been really close before, seemed miles away. Bombette and Ray paddled back towards shore, checked back in with their reference points, caught a wave in and celebrated another epic session with a well deserved glass of red wine.
Corriente? Check!

La corriente (noun, feminine)

koh-rryehn-teh (IPA: ko-rjen-te)

current

Water moving into a certain direction. Rip currents generally flow away from the beach back into the ocean, side shore currents flow parallel to the beach. Beginner surfers fear them, experienced surfers love them.

Viento, what a love-hate relationship!
We love him when he blows onto our oceans.
Really, really far away. We hate him when he
blows exactly where we want to surf.

Wrapped up in a warm jacket and a beanie
she was sitting on one of Lanzarote's beaches.
Local surf guide Melly was in the water with
the surf trip crew while Angie had stayed
outside and filmed their waves. It was a pretty
windy day, the end of January can be a bit
'harsh' sometimes.

It was the end of the session and Angie had
just stored her camera into the backpack.
Team dog Rainbow was sitting next to her.
Two of her students just left the water when it
happened. A small tornado had formed right
on the shore, right where her students had
just left the ocean.

And the tornado was moving inland pretty
fast, catching her students in the way.
Angie threw herself on top of Rainbow and
her camera and screamed: tornaaaado.
But it was too late already. The tornado had
lifted two of her students into the air, spitting
them and the surfboards back onto the
beach.

After a few seconds it was over. Everyone was
covered in sand, but luckily no one was hurt.
Laughing about what had just happened,
they finished the day with a great story to tell.
Viento, a love-hate relationship!

El viento (noun, masculine)

byehn-toh (IPA: bjen-to)

wind

One of nature's wonders, a movement of air blowing in a particular direction onto our planet. When blowing on the ocean's surface wind creates waves, our objects of desire. Ranges from a light breeze to a powerful hurricane.

There are millions of ways to leave a wave. Every surfer has a favourite way of finishing a wave. Often depending on the surf level, it looks controlled and stylish.

These are the most common **salidas**:

The good old wipeout
The fall onto your board
The dive head first
The Arschbombe (bum first)
The kick out over the wave
The backflip

She was the unofficial master of epic **salidas**. Using the lip of the wave as a ramp, Linda threw herself behind the wave. She straightened her body into a plank, extended her arms forward and in an explosive moment catapulted herself into the air. Her long curly hair followed her in a wavelike motion, and as the adrenaline pumped through Linda's body she let out a joyful scream, claiming her wave to be a success.

Everyone in the water had to smile instantly. Surfing really brings together a special type of people. Linda didn't mind. She simply enjoyed playing with the energy of the waves.

By the way, her particular way of finishing the wave makes it easy to identify Linda in the water. Even from a distance or on a cloudy day you know it's her.
How is that for a signature **salida**?

La salida (noun, feminine)

sah-lee-dah (IPA: sa-li-ða)

exit

Way of finishing a wave. Can be done stylish and with grace.
Often accompanied by a claim and scream. Also what to ask
for when you want to get back to the beach.

We have all watched surf movies. We might even follow the Championship Tour from the World Surf League and hype ourselves on all those crazy **maniobras** out there. It is totally impressive and next level unreal what professional surfers are able to do with their surfboards.

In surfing it is important to set ourselves goals. Like which board we would like to surf one day, which wave to explore, and also which **maniobra** to learn.

She had also set herself a goal, one that she had defined for herself as being reachable: Miri wanted to surf a wave straight to the beach. Easy done you think, but not if your head is facing the ocean. Seriously? Yep. Her goal was to surf in reverse gear.

Miri first learned how to catch a whitewash straight to the beach. Great. Next step, she thought, but turned out that shuffling her feet to face the other way wasn't as easy as she had imagined. Miri didn't give up and on her last day in Galicia, it finally happened.

She took off on a wave and followed the whitewash to the shore, shuffled her feet and turned her head and body. Woooow, that a view!! It was everything Miri had imagined. A loud: beepbeepbeep reverse gear sound came from her lips.

So here we go: the best surfer is the one having the most fun, not the best **maniobra**! And sometimes it pays off to not take yourself too seriously.

La maniobra (noun, feminine)

mah-nyoh-brah (IPA: ma-njo-βra)

trick / maneuver

Chain of movements that we execute to make our surfboard take advantage of the wave's full potential. Includes (but not limited to) bottom and top turns, cutback and getting barreled.

Just like any other sport, surfing has rules. An important one is the priority rule. Generally, the surfer sitting closest to the peak (the breaking part of the wave) has priority. Sometimes the surfer taking off at the peak hasn't been seen and the drop in wasn't intentional. In the unfortunate reality though, the priority rule is often overlooked or ignored. This can result in accidents, dinged boards and bad vibes in the water.

She had been surfing for a while now and had progressed to a skill level where she could easily catch waves. Nonetheless, Bombette still felt a bit intimidated by the mostly male dominated line-up and wasn't sure where her place was.

Her surf coach had shown her a way to clear her head game and gain more confidence: **voy**! Bombette was willing to give it a go. When the next wave approached, she started paddling, but so did the surfer next to her. Bombette knew she was closer to the peak and therefore had priority but instead of giving up and doubting herself she took some extra deep strokes.

The surfer next to her was still paddling for the wave, totally ignoring her effort and intention to catch the wave. Knowing she was in the right and believing in her abilities, Bombette took off on the wave and yelled a serious: **VOY!** The surfer next to her looked puzzled but pulled back and Bombette could finish the wave to the beach. Great way of communication and an incredible confidence boost.

Voy! (verb, first form singular)

voy (IPA: vɔɪ)

I go!

A useful expression, often screamed, to inform nearby surfers last minute that you A. are willing to take the wave you are paddling for and B. will take it no matter what. Please note: not taking the wave you claimed or wiping out will result in you enjoying the rest of your session from the channel.

Surfing is a selfish sport. By the end of the day, it's only you and the wave. Still, there are other surfers in the water with you. Rule number one in surfing is give respect to gain respect. And that includes letting waves pass by and also releasing waves when you feel that:

A. you are not 100% sure you will catch the wave
B. someone else is better positioned that you are
C. you know you are going to nosedive

The best way to let other surfers know that you are not going to catch the wave is by yelling: dale, dale!

As a confident surfer, and unofficial Gummiflischen-Guru, he used it frequently. Joshiño hardly ever went anywhere without his foamie. Surfing a buoyant foam board made it easy for him to catch waves.

He was paddling for a wave when he saw Miri aiming for the same one. Wanting her to have the wave, he paddled over and tried to help her get into the wave. Everything looked fine, ohh noo, Miri went straight into nosedive mode.

Miri also realized what was happening and managed to shout a quick **dale, dale** before going over the falls. With one more stroke Joshiño was able to catch the wave, popped up and smoothly landed sideways laying on the board. That was his trademark move after all.

Stoked about Miri´s textbook surf attitude, Joshiños paddled back out and remembered why he loved surfing so much. In the end it is all about sharing the stoke.

Dale, dale! (phrase, imperative)

dah-leh, dah-leh (IPA: da-le, da-le)

You go!

A useful expression to make friends in the line-up and smooth the locals. Basically expresses you are not going to take the wave you are paddling for and releasing the wave to other surfers to be surfed.

Close your eyes and imagine a wave building up in front of you. You think you are in the perfect take-off zone. But surprise, the wave moves differently than you expected and now breaks right in front of you. What do you do? Your best bet is the pato. A technique to submerge yourself and your surfboard under the wave and use the circular motion of the waves energy to get spit out behind the wave.

She couldn't imagine how she would ever be able to do it. Having just started surfing on a bulky foamie, Miri really doubted the physics behind this move, but she was going to find out soon.

She was on a surf coaching trip on Tenerife and surf coach Angie had scheduled a **pato** practice session at the pool of their homebase for the afternoon. Angie first explained the dynamic and technique of pushing your board underwater and then got prepared to demonstrate it in the pool. Joined by one of the surf crew guys the two happily jumped into the outside pool. Only to jump out straight away, trembling to the bones.

Turned out that the pool averaged at around 5°C ice block style temperature. No wonder, as the house was located on 1.200m altitude, in plain January. A fact that they had overlooked.

Content about not having to deal with the **pato** just yet, Miri smiled and handed Angie a hot cup of tea.

El pato (noun, masculine)

pah-toh (IPA: pa-to)

duckdive

Special skill to submerge yourself and the surfboard under the oncoming waves. When executed correctly, an easy way to reach the peak. When executed without the right technique and timing, it often results in an embarrassing washing machine.

Communication is a skill, and an easy way to avoid misunderstandings and trouble in general. Even though gestures and facial expressions are a big part of making us understood, words are still our main weapon of choice. But what happens if you don't speak the same language as your opponent?

She had been surfing on the Canary Islands a few times and had already picked up some essential Spanish words. That's why Miri felt positive about being able to communicate in the water. However, one day on Tenerife, Miri hesitated. She had watched the surfers in the water for a while and discovered that sometimes they would shout something at each other. There was a clearly marked peak with waves breaking left and right. She approached local surf guide Emilio Slater and asked what was going on.

Emilio explained that the surfers were shouting: **izquierda / derecha** (left/right), to let the other surfers know which direction in the wave they were planning
to take.

Prepared with a couple of new Spanish words and the confidence to be able to announce her line in the water, Miri too, paddled out. When her first wave approached, she realized she was in the perfect position for going right. Emilio Slater was next to her, paddling for the same wave. Miri put on her best smiley face, confidently yelled: **dereeecha**, took off on the wave and surfed it all the way down to the beach. Emilio, proud of his student, went for the **izquierda** and shredded it to bits. How good does it feel to share waves?

Izquierda / Derecha
(substantive, feminine)

ees-kyehr-dah / deh-reh-chah (IPA: iθ-kjeɾ-ða /de-ɾe-tʃa)

left / right

Verbal indication about which direction of the wave you intent to surf. Avoids confusion and bad vibes in the water.

Equipo de surf

- surf equipment -

A **tabla** comes in all forms, sizes and colors. Most beginner surfers start off renting surfboards, it is a big investment after all. But let's face it, surfing a different **tabla** every time you hit the ocean can slow down your learning process.

The first board she had owned. It's a feeling Ray won't ever forget. After having surfed rentals for years, she figured it was time for her own **tabla**. While the size and shape had been her main priority, she was also looking for something stylish. And finally, Ray found it. The perfect **tabla**. The perfect shape. The perfect size. And yes, the perfect style. Please meet ORKI, her master of the waves.

From this day on, Ray never went anywhere near the ocean without taking Orki. And of course, she also accompanied Ray on her surf trip to Galicia, where she joined a fun group of cool surfers and enjoyed the luxury of being dropped off at the best waves every day. Total stoke.

Until, one morning, Orki was nowhere to be found. Ray slightly freaked. Had somebody taken her overnight? Did she forget her on the beach? What happened to her? Ray frantically searched everywhere, screaming: *¿Dónde está mi **tabla**?* (Where is my surfboard?)

And then it hit her. Maybe someone had already loaded her into the surf van? Maybe she was cuddling up with the other boards inside Ramon's van? And that's exactly where Ray found her Orki, her beloved **tabla**. Let´s go surfing!

La tabla (de surf) (noun, feminine)

tah - blah (IPA: ta-βla)

surfboard

The magic board that makes it possible for us to glide along the face of the wave. Word has it, that some people even nickname their surfboards.

Galicia, Spain's most north western region, isn't particularly known as a sunny beach holiday destination. Thinking of Galicia, you probably imagine a rugged coastline, howling winds and pouring down rain.

And it's true, that's what it's like in the winter months, and especially up on the North Coast. What you probably don't know is that Galicia's west coast has its own microclimate with loads of sunshine and warm weather. Crazy, right?

Well, Bombette, Lindis and Miri didn't know either about the sunny days awaiting them and surfed four weeks straight, all day long. Although the sun was warm, the Atlantic water temperature ranged at around only 18°C, making a 4.3mm **traje** a necessity. This neoprene bodysuit not only protected their bodies from the exposure to cold water temperatures but also to the exposure of the sun. Resulting in only their faces, hands and feet nicely tanned by the Galician sun.

The longer Bombette, Lindis and Miri stayed in Galicia, the more they wondered about people staring at them in the nearby supermarket. Sure, there weren't too many international tourists in that area but still. Until they caught a reflection of themselves, wearing short summer clothes and they quickly realized how funny they looked to the local non-surfer population: tanned hands, feet and head, and an epic **traje** tanline.

El traje (de neopreno)
(noun, masculine)

trah - heh (IPA: tɾa-χe)

wetsuit

A full body suit that protects our bodies from exposure to cold water and prolonged sunshine. Made originally from neoprene but nowadays more sustainable options are available. Often leaves an epic tan line to show off with.

We surfers are generally low key. Often it's just us, the waves and our surfboard. The more equipment we have, the longer it takes to jump into the waves. However, when it comes to safety in the water, we might have to add an extra bit of equipment.

He was running a surf school in the Northwest of Ireland. A stunning countryside and epic waves had drawn Lee or "Good Old Lee" as we've come to know him, to this corner of the world. He loved sharing this place with other surfers and was stoked for the annual November surf trip group to be there once again.

One morning conditions looked great for one of the hidden back beaches. Hidden might be the right word as you have to find the right turn off, drive through a local farm, open a few gates and finally park in the middle of a field. The crew was hyped. So many sheep around. They got suited up and looked surprised: no ocean in sight.Good Old Lee explained that they would have to cross another couple of fields to reach the dunes.

As usual, he handed out his red shredder **licras** to put on top of the wetsuits. They were making their way through the first field when something caught Good Old Lee's eye. Wooow, that was a big sheep approaching the group. But wait, it wasn't a sheep. Nooo, it was a bull. Racing towards one of his students, clearly being in love with the red **licra**. Ruuuuun, Good Old Lee screamed, started running and quickly closed the gate to the next field behind him and his students. How is that for an explosive warm-up?

La licra (noun, feminine)

lee-krah (IPA: li-kɾa)

lycra shirt

Flexible shirt, short or long sleeved, worn by surfers.
Generally used as sun protection or for extra warmth. Also
used by surf schools to identify their ´herd´ in the water.
Neon colours preferred.

When we surf, we are exposed to all sorts of natural conditions. There is the wind, the water temperature and also the sun. For some of us, lucky enough to live near the ocean and surf every day, it is essential to protect ourselves from mother nature's forces.

She was living on Fuerteventura, one of the Canary Islands. Cold surely wasn't an issue here, surfing in a shorty for 6 months of the year was Angie's happy reality. The downside of having loads of sun was the constant exposure to the sun's rays. Any sort of protection, meaning caps, clothing or **crema solar** were essential. Angie's daily morning routine included brushing her teeth, washing her face, and applying the first coat of **crema solar**.

But that wasn't enough to protect her skin during all the hours spend in the water. Angie figured she needed something more powerful. That's when she discovered zink, or better zink oxide crema solar. A powerful blocker to fight the sun's UVA and UVB rays.

Wow, that felt a lot better. Good news, zink is now available in eco-friendly and colorful versions. Angie absolutely loved the pink, what a detail. For years she was known for her pink warrior stripes. Funny fact: even though it is great that zink sticks to your face, it is really hard to scrub off at night.
Prepare yourself!

La crema solar (noun, feminine)

kreh-mah soh-lahr (IPA: kɾe-ma so-laɾ)

s u n s c r e e n

Protects us from the sun's nasty rays. Apply generously
at your face, ears and neck when wearing a wetsuit. Use
coloured zink sunscreen to create a hulk effect and gain more
respect in the line-up.

A surfboard is generally made of foam, resin or epoxy resin, leaving it with a slippery surface. Which then again makes it hard for us surfers to keep a stable balance while riding the wave.

Luckily for us, at some point, someone figured out that if you apply **parafina** to the top of the surface of the surfboard, it gives you grip and stops your feet from sliding off. Experienced snowboarders or skiers might think that's weird, as they use **parafina** for exactly the opposite: less friction and more speed when applied to the bottom of the board.

She had grown up close to the mountains and had never questions the **parafina** on the bottom of the board technique. But since Miri had started surfing she was getting good at applying heaps of wax on the top of her foamie. One day she was waxing her surfboard, but unfortunately, had underestimated the strong Spanish sun. Her carefully prepared **parafina** pattern turned into a liquid sludge within a couple of minutes.

Puzzled and a little bit embarrassed Miri went to local surf guide Ramonski and asked him for a second piece of wax. With a smile he pulled out an oversized surprise egg. Was he making fun of her? Miri carefully opened the egg and started laughing. Turned out that Ramonski had known about the **parafina's** reaction with the sun and was hiding his **parafina** in the oversized egg. What a surprise!

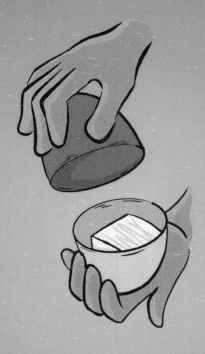

La parafina (noun, feminine)

pah-rah-fee-nah (IPA: pa-ɾa-fi-na)

surfboard wax

Used for grip on the surfboard. The name originates from the former main ingredient of surfboard wax. Luckily, more ecological options to create grip on your surfboard are now available. Opt for wax made locally and support small businesses.

In order to become a surf coach you have to make your way through various courses. Depending on where you live, different qualifications are accepted. In Spain, one generally does a course run by the regional surf federation.

They both wanted to be surf coaches. Having had experience teaching others how to surf, both Melly and Angie now wanted to take the next step and become qualified surf instructors. They signed up for the level I course run by the Canarian Surf Federation, held on the island of Tenerife. They had never met before, but quickly became friends when they realized they were the only non-local girls in the course.

In their free time they went for a surf in the South of the island. Melly was a native Spanish speaker, born in Argentina and bred on Lanzarote. Angie was a blond guiri, a tourist who got stuck on Fuerteventura. Even though Angie had a decent level of Spanish, mix-ups did happen.

They were getting changed in the carpark, ready to hit the waves. Angie was struggling with one of her quillas and mumbling to herself. Melly approached her and asked if she could help. Yes, she could help. ¡Ayudame con mi quillo por favor, Angie said. Quillo, Melly thought?? But Quillo wasn't even there. Quillo was a surfer dude from Las Palmas who was also joining the course.

Looking puzzled, Melly realized that Angie had confused the final letter and was talking about the **quilla** of her surfboard. With a great giggle they made their way into the waves.

La quilla (noun, feminine)

kee-yah(IPA:ki-ja)

surfboard fin

Fins attached to the back of a surfboard improve stability, give speed and control and act as a pivot point. They vary in set-up: single fin, twin fin, thruster and quad, are the most popular ones. Made of plastic, fibre and/or resin. Have a direct impact on your performance.

Competencias sociales

- social skills -

The oceans cover the biggest part of our planet. Our little playground at the shore is really just a grain of sand compared to the size of the ocean. Even though we think that we have control about the ocean and the waves, let's face it: we are simply visitors in an environment it isn't ours to live in.

He had figured out for himself that he wasn't alone in the water. Well, as Joshiño was running a surf school in Galicia he really wasn't alone in the water much. But even on the days he went surfing by himself, Joshiño could feel the presence of the ocean's inhabitants. What a feeling!

Like every year in May a group of surf trippers had come over to his coastline, and Joshiño made sure they were at the right spot at the right time. This day he had taken the group to a beach a few miles up the coast. Here he could feel it even more, the connection to the ocean. This day he felt it even stronger than usual. Something was about to happen, he knew.

Excited, Joshiño entered the water and paddled out to the line-up. Then they arrived, No! Not his students, but a whole gang of dolphins. As if he had known, he felt a strong urge to hug them but instead he simply watched them play in the waves and said out loud: **Hola ¿que tal,** chicos??
The answer came quickly, a big happy splash right next to him.

Hola, ¿qué tal? (phrase)

loh-lah keh tahl (IPA: o-la ke tal)

Hi, how are you?

Phrase to acknowledge someone's presence. No direct answer is expected but can result in a friendly conversation and more waves. Combined with a smile it can be an ice-breaker.

Everyone knows the shaka, the internationally recognized hand signal to greet another surfer. The shaka has been around since the beginning of surfing but why not shake up things a little bit?

Being of a bubbly personality, she thought about how to leave a positive first impression when arriving at the line-up. Ray was going to spend a few weeks in Galicia, Northwest Spain, after all. Being a travelling surfer, Ray respected the locals in the water and wanted to make sure to pay them the respect they deserved. However, she couldn't really figure out how to say hello in the water.

One day, watching the waves and waiting for the tide to drop, she was talking to surfcoach Ramonski. He was enthusiastically talking about a town called Rachel (her real name) in Nevada, USA. Ramonski had watched a documentary about this rather strange town with a population of only 54.
Seemed like in Rachel there had been some UFO sightings and there was ongoing research about extra-terrestrial activities.

And there it was. The inspiration Ray had been waiting for. And just like that, her new signature **saludo** was born. Tried and proved in and outside the water Ray now felt confident to conquer the local line-up.

El saludo (noun, masculine)

sahl-oo-doh (IPA: sa-lu-ðo)

greeting

Proper way to greet when arriving at a line-up. Takes people by surprise, generally puts a smile on their faces, plus they know you come in peace.

Learning to surf is an exciting journey. In the beginning you will learn to master a big bulky board and then master the waves. Having other surfers around you during your learning process, adds an extra level of difficulty.

On this sunny Galician day there were more surfers in the water than usual. He was in the water with the surf trip crew, making sure they all caught waves. This was Ramonski's local wave so he was relaxed about the situation, but suddenly Miri turned to him for **ayuda**.

Miri: Ramonski?
Ramonski: Yes Miri?
Miri: I am scared that I catch a wave and crash into somebody.
Ramonski: Relax. This generally won't happen. But just in case, don't worry, I am here with you, and I am always prepared.

A. I know where all the close by hospitals are
B. I have a first aid kit in my car
C. And if everything goes wrong, I have a shovel.

With a terrified face Miri quickly paddled further out sea. That was not the **ayuda** she had hoped for. Ramonski smirked about his joke and Miri´s face, then caught the next wave. Happy to help!

Serious smallprint: Surfing in an extreme sport taking place in nature. Accidents can happen and it is better to be prepared. While HELP is an internationally recognized word, it might not be recognized by the person who could potentially save your life. Please always learn the local expression!

La ayuda (noun, feminine)

ah - yoo- dah (IPA: a-ɟu-ða)

help

Hopefully we will never have to ask for serious help. Use
ayuda also when you forgot your leash/wax at home and want
to borrow some.

It is awesome to have a local. A place you know inside out and where people know you. A local wave. A local surfshop. And also, a local bar. And even if you haven't been born in the area, one still gets attached to places and people.

And yep, she felt attached to Galicia. For Angie, it was her favourite place on mainland Europe. A place where she magically felt she belonged and kept returning to year after year. Angie didn't think she was a local, but she was stoked to recognize friendly faces in and outside the water.

Especially in her favourite bar, which she lovingly called 'Abierto todo el año' (open all year round). After a surf in the mellow waves of La Curva, Angie just loved sitting on the terrace, watching the waves roll in and enjoy an ice-cold drink.

Her favourite waiter, who was never shy of a cheeky comment, spoiled Angie with a freshly poured **cerveza**. Served in a chilled glass. Have you ever tried a **cerveza** served in a pre-chilled glass? It's epic!

And there she was, zipping away and thinking: a perfect end to yet another perfect day. Gracias!

La cerveza (noun, feminine)

sehr-beh-sah (IPA: seɾ-βe-sa)

beer

An alcoholic drink made of malt and hops. Best enjoyed
ice cold, in a pre frozen glass with ocean view. Best served
straight after an epic surf.

Surf holidaying in a foreign country you are exposed to a different culture and language. That's part of the fun and makes travelling really exciting. After a few days in one place you will start recognizing the same words being used over and over again. Hanging out in Spain you will hear the word **hostia** wherever you go.

That's what she thought, too. Seemed to Miri that hostia could be used in pretty much any combination. So she decided why not, let's go for it and show off a bit with a newly acquired word. Without a care Miri started using hostia in front of pretty much everything. As it turned out, this can get you into quite a bit of trouble, too.

Ramonski: Miri!
Miri: Si, Ramonski?
Ramonski: You know there's a different meaning when you add the plural 's' to guapo?
Miri: What do you mean?
*Ramonski: You see, when you look at the wave you can say: **Hostia, qué guapo**! But when you say: **Hostia, qué guapos**, you are going fishing!*

Needless to say that Miri went back to using **hostia** without any further additions.

Hostia, qué guapo
(noun, feminine & adjective, singular)
ohs-thya, khe gwah poh (IPA: os-tja, ke gwa-po)

so pretty / cool

Hostia, qué guapos
(noun, feminine & adjective, plural)
ohs-thya, khe gwah pohs (IPA: os-tja, ke gwa-pos)

nice boys / sexy people

Universal expressions. Can be used in pretty much every
situation. In and outside the water. For waves, surroundings,
surfboards, hot guys etc.

Without doubt one of the most useful phrases to learn in a foreign language is how to say that you don't understand a word that is being thrown at you.

She was on one of her surf trips on Gran Canaria. After an epic surf session on the East Coast Angie had decided to drive to the South to buy a pair of flip flop in one of the touristy shops in one of the touristy towns. Why she had decided to do that in the first place is a story of its own. Three of her surf trip chicas were up for a detour.

After successfully completing the flip flop mission they checked the map for the way back to their house in the North and decided to take a road right through the middle of the island. What they didn't take into account was that Gran Canaria elevates up to nearly 2000m. Making it a long journey back home.

They took a pit stop in a picturesque little mountain town and parked their car right next to the small supermarket in the pedestrianized area. Two of the chicas stayed in the car. If someone came to complain they were meant to simply say:
'no entiendo' (I don't understand).

Angie hopped into the shop but when she returned and approached the car she heard the surf chicas screaming: no nintendo, no nintendo'. Seemed like the girls had improvised after forgetting the correct expression. Laughing about just another funny memory to share they continued their journey back to the homebase.

No entiendo (verb, negation)

noh ehn-tyehn-doh (IPA: no en-tjen-do)

I don't understand

Expresses that you have no idea what the other person is talking about. Can be freely used if you don't understand or simply don't want to understand.

Mundo surfero

- surfers world -

Surfing, like any other sport, has rules that we play by. Even though nowadays they are not getting taught properly, or are being simply ignored, they are still there.

Here are the most important **reglas del surf** for you to remember:

- Don't drop into someone else's wave
- Paddle wide to stay alive
(use the channel to get back out)
- Don't throw your surfboard
- Communicate
- Respect the locals, wait your turn

On her local beach in Lanzarote there can be quite a crowd sometimes. Loads of surf schools and free surfers are battling for the waves on the beautiful
6 km long beach. So it was even more important for Melly to pass on the reglas de surf to her students.

Her friend from Fuerteventura had come over with her surf trip crew. Just like on the first trip, Melly was responsible for picking the right time and the right spot for the crew to surf. Easily done, as she knew all the beaches and conditions.

But throwing a group of people into the ocean comes with responsibility. That's why Melly made sure to have explained the **reglas del surf** to everyone. No dropping, no board throwing, using the channels, communication and respect! Well done!

Las reglas del surf
(noun, feminine, plural)

rreh-glahs deh soorf (IPA: re-ɣla de suɾf)

surfing etiquette

The rules we live by as surfers. Rule number one of surfing:
give respect to gain respect!

For some high-profile athletes surfing is a career and a serious competitive sport. For most of us however, surfing is something we simply love filling our days with. Having fun in the water is an essential part of the whole surfing experience.

Sure, we all want to catch heaps of waves and glide along the waves face as many times as possible. Pure adrenaline. But how cool is it to share perfect waves and jokes with your friends in the water? Isn't it all about fun in the first place?

That's what they thought, too. A decent groundswell was forecasted to hit Galicia's west coast that day so Miri and Lindis were sitting in the line-up waiting for waves. Waiting for a high period swell to push in means loads of time between sets. So sure, there was time for some **tonterías**.

That's what they thought, at least. And while Miri and Lindis had been busy trying to push each other off the surfboard, their surfcoach saw the first big set building up. They heard her scream: seeeeet, but it was too late. Off guard, Miri and Lindis took the first set wave on the head and ate the whole set after that. When washed up onto the beach they laughed, high fived, paddled back out and kept going with their **tonterías**. Some of us just never grow up. ;)

Las tonterías (noun, feminine, plural)

tohn-teh-ree-ahs (IPA: ton-te-ɾi-as<)

nonsense / Schabernack

Fooling around in the water with friends / partner / future prospect. Generally includes laughing, pushing off the board, opening the leash etc.

Marea alta and **Marea baja** are a natural phenomenon. For us as surfers, it's essential to know about them as many surf spots only work on specific tides. Often overlooked is the so called tidal range, which is the difference (in meters) between **marea alta** and **marea baja**. Measured at the lowest astronomical tide, the chart datum, this tidal range can get us into quite a bit of trouble when ignored.

The fog was dense, she could hear the waves breaking but couldn't see a thing. Angie had never surfed at this beach in Wales before and was too insecure to paddle out by herself so she waited for someone to turn up. And she was lucky. Suddenly a few vans showed up, some guys in business suits hopped out and got changed into wetsuits. She felt like she was in a movie.

Angie quickly ran over and asked if they would mind if she paddled out with them. They didn't. She jumped into her wetsuit and for the next 1 ½ hrs shredded in the fog. Just when she was ready to head back to the beach, the fog lifted and Angie frowned: the beach was soooo far away. How did that happen? There hadn't been a strong current to have drifted that much. Preparing herself for an exhausting and long paddle back to the beach Angie asked the dude sitting next to her about something she had completely forgotten to check: the tidal range. He answered with a smirky smile: 'yeah, it's a bit epic right now, it's about 8m!'

As you can imagine, that was the last time ever Angie forgot to check the tidal range!

La marea alta / baja
(nouns, feminine)

mah-reh-ah ahl-tah / bah-hah (IPA: ma-ɾe-a al-ta / ba-χa)

hightide / lowtide

Tidal movement of the world's oceans. Mostly semi-diurnal,
2 x high tide and 2 x low tide per day. 6 hrs and 12,5 min
between each tide results in changing tide times every day.
Important info for spot checks.

As surfers we love to be outdoors and we care about our planet. Unfortunately, not everyone feels this way. Often local governments and private investors care more about their profits than the environment. That explains horrible jetties, houses and factories being built right on the shoreline. Having a direct influence on the ocean floor and water quality, destroying once epic waves.

Good news is that more and more local communities fight for the protection of their coastline. Really lucky ones manage to get their wave protected as a **reserva mundial de surf**. Making any further construction development impossible.

She felt strongly about the environment. One day in Galicia Miri had decided to skip the morning surf session. They had pulled up to a beautiful empty beach and she had decided to stay in the car park. There was a little stretch of grass right in front of the surf van, so Miri took the sun umbrella, surf trip dog Rainbow and wrapped herself in one of the board socks. A little siesta wouldn't hurt.

Miri instantly fell asleep on the grass, only to be woken up by a council environmental officer. Screaming into her face: No camping! No perros! No sombrilla! No siesta! Quickly she packed up everything and jumped back into the surf van. Miri guessed he had mistaken her for an overnight guest. And even though she wasn't in a **reserve mundial de surf**, she was indeed in a natural park. When the others returned and she told her story, the joke was on her and her new 'boyfriend'.

La reserva mundial de surf
(noun, feminine)

rreh-sehr-bah moon-dyahl deh soorf (IPA: re-seɾ-βa mun-djal de surf)

world surf reserve

A sacred place of extraordinary wave quality. Officially protected by laws from constructions or any other human destruction.

Everyone sets priorities in their lives. This generally involves a secure job, a stable relationship, and a cosy home. For us surfers however, all this comes, with quite a gap, behind one particular thing: surfing waves.

Most of us weren't born like that. It's just something that happened at one point in our timeline. How? We never really knew. It might be the connection with nature, the adrenaline rush of the wave or the community.

Didn't matter their journeys but they all lived their lives chasing waves. And that's how they ended up at the same beach, at the same time, surfing the same waves in Galicia.

Angie was running a surf coaching trip. They were travelling along mainland Europe looking for waves and beautiful places. Angie was living in a rented holiday house in walking distance to the beach. They were living in their van, right at the beach. Angie working as a surfcoach. They were working as a digital marketing freelancer and longboard master coach.

They were friends. And stoked to be sharing waves and epic moments. In the end that's what it is all about when living the **vida surfera**.

Ps: no doubt that team dog Rainbow is the one most enjoying this lifestyle!

La vida surfera (noun, feminine)

bee-dah suhrf-eh-rah (IPA: bi-ða səf-e-ɾa)

surfer life

Type of lifestyle that is centred around chasing waves. Often involves being on the road and living minimalized. Generally awarded with an extremely high wavecount.

Where you have waves you are most likely to find an **escuela de surf**. That's pretty cool because they can provide you with surf lessons, any sort of surf equipment and even more important: local knowledge.

But when it comes to **escuelas de surf**, location is not everything. Maybe you have noticed how they can vary in quality. A good indicator for a quality school is the general appearance of the school, the equipment (i.e. surfboards) and the staff.

He had found the perfect location for an **escuela de surf**. A small holiday town on the Irish coast, bustling in the summer months, nice and quiet in the off season. There were loads of different beaches in a short driving distance, making all year-round surf lessons possible.

Good Old Lee and his surf buddy and business partner Duncan had started off with renting a small shop right next to the village square. But when the old bank building was up for grabs, they didn't hesitate, and moved onto the main street. Painting it in blue and white it now looked pretty and welcoming for a bank, oops, sorry, a surf shop.

Now imagine how confusing it would be for any bank robber in spe to arrive at the old bank, in full gear and ready to go. To find a surf shop filled with boards and cool gear, plus Good Old Lee sitting outside.
Caution: he might even invite you in for a steaming hot coffee.

La escuela de surf (noun, feminine)

ehs-kweh-lah deh soorf (IPA: es-kwe-la de suɾf)

surf school

A place where you can sign up for surf lessons and meet cool people. Can generally be found close to a beach with waves. Often offers surf equipment to rent and surf stuff to buy.

The sun and the **luna** have a direct influence on our oceans: the tides. And while the sun is bigger, the luna is closer to us and is therefore playing a more important role. The gravitational pull of the **luna** generates the so called tidal force. Forcing the earth to bulge on the side closest to the **luna**. However, it also bulges at the other site, making the oceans rise.

He was running a surf school and a lifesaving academy on Lanzarote. During the past years Paul had explained the tides phenomenon a million times. And so he explained it once more to a group of surf trippers who had signed up for a 'lifesaving for surfers' session with him.

They seemed like a funny enough group, so Paul decided to also tell his theory on werewolves: In ancient times poor homeless people were being kicked out of towns and villages. Leaving nowhere to live but the woods. Here they lived away from society, no need to shave or wear pretty clothes. Still, somehow, they had to survive and eat. The occasional sheep was stolen and killed.

Back then, farmers had blamed other animals for the death of the sheep. Until one **luna** llena (full moon) when a big hairy something was spotted eating a sheep in the bright light. The farmers assumed it to be a werewolf: half man – half wolf. A myth was born. Truth is, it simply had been one of the homeless people living in the woods.

Everyone laughed. What a great story. Paul loved making the whole luna-tide issue a lot more interesting.

La luna (noun, feminine)

loo-nah (IPA: lu-na)

moon

The planet circling around us. Responsible for sleepless nights, midnight surf sessions and differences in the tidal range.

While we as surfers are stoked to spend our days in the **medio ambiente** we also fear for its health. Global warming and pollution are threatening not only our entire planet but especially the ecosystem of our oceans.

As surfers we have the unwritten responsibility to leave the beach cleaner than we have found it. It is a natural urge to thank mother nature for letting us play in her waves. As travelling surfers, we also have the chance to have an influence on the local community receiving us.

She travelled to Ghana to surf. Angie got there a week before her surf trip crew. She had arrived in the middle of the night and woke up early by the sounds of the jungle. Angie took her surfboard and ran down to the beach. Warm water, epic waves and super friendly locals. It was paradise, she thought.

But there was something wrong with paradise. On the beach and also in the water, was a lot of rubbish and plastic bits. What a shock. Surely there was something she could do to help. In the water one of the local surfers had told Angie about a group of locals who, twice a week, cleaned the beaches and the main street of the little village. The next day, instead of surfing into sunrise, Angie joined the group and did her little bit to give back to this amazing little community and the **medio ambiente**.

PS: amazing work by BBCC (Busua Beach Community Caretakers). Please support them!

El medio ambiente (noun, masculine)

meh-dyoh-ahm-byehn-teh (IPA: me-ðjo-am-bjen-te)

environment

The fragile area surrounding us where all living and non-living things can exist in their natural ways. Provides us with fresh air, food and epic waves. Please protect it!

Doesn't matter your level of surfing, falling off your surfboard will always happen. In the beginning it's getting ripped off the board by the whitewash, later it's falling down a big, hollow wall of water.

He was guiding a surf trip group which came over to Tenerife, Emilio's beloved island. The first couple of days he had taken them to mellow waves, easy done. On the third day however, he decided it was time to get more serious.

Miri was one of the girls on the team. Having next to no surfing experience, she made up for her lack of skills with pure motivation. But right now, Emilio saw pure terror on her face: where had the mellow waves disappeared to? In shock she stared at walls of water moving into the bay.

Emilio knew she would be ok, as she paddled out with the rest of the group. Not long until he called her into her first wave. She did use every skill she possessed but bad news: there she was, free falling down what felt like a gigantic mountain of water.

When she resurfaced next to him, Emilio smiled and said: 'chica, what a **caída**! But don't worry, you are not going to die today, you can die tomorrow. Still, remember, today, we are here for surfing, not for watching fish.' Exhausted but laughing about herself free falling head first, she paddled for the channel. And then did it all over again.

La caída (noun, feminine)

kah-ee-dah (IPA: ka-i-ða)

wipe out

A wave gone wrong. Generally involves you head first in the
water and your board doing loops on the surface.

A body of water covers about 71% of our planet. It's called the **océano**. Or better the océanos. Even though it's one big lake, it gets divided into the Atlantic, Pacific, Indian and Arctic. Sometimes they even add the Antarctic.

There is something mystical about this vast lake. It's size, it's power, the inability to predict it. Ever heard of freak waves for example?

They were sitting at the shore of their homebreak. It's been an epic month Angie and Miri had just spent in Galicia. The waves had been rolling in all day, at just the right size. Countless waves were surfed, the stoke level was high. The sun was slowly setting, a dark red coloured the horizon. A perfect end to a perfect trip.

Angie and Miri were reminiscing in memories from the past few weeks. What a group it had been again this year. There is just something about the **océano**. Somehow it manages to bring together the best groups of people.

As they waved goodbye to the setting sun and the last waves of the day they were already thinking about next year. Same time, same place. With a warmed heart they thought: sea you later, beloved **oceáno**!

El océano (noun, masculine)

oh-seh-ah-noh (IPA: o-θe-a-no)

ocean

Our favourite place to be on this planet. Luckily the oceans cover 70% of the world's surface. Loads of space for waves being generated, loads of salt water to nourish our wave addiction.

Thanks for joining us on our journey down memory lane. Illustrating and writing this book has been a challenge but what a fun one. Countless changes later we are proud to have created a book that will hopefully help you navigate a Spanish speaking line-up. And maybe, you´ve learned the odd bit about surfing, too. A big gracias goes out to every single one who has been part of our journey: **Annette, Emilio, Josh, Lee, Linda, Melina, Paul, Rahel and Ramon.**

Some special words from the creators:

Angie (texts)
I would like to shout out a special thank you to:

Dani, for listening to me constantly raving about this book,
Ian, for the proof read,
Dad & **Annette**, for the legal advice,
all the beautiful **NOMB Surfers**, who made most of these trips possible in the first place
and last but not least to **Miris** for being the incredible artist and friend she is. Epic journey!

Miri (illustrations & design)
Surfing has changed my view of life in ways I could never have imagined, and as an artist, inspires me in my daily work. Big thanks to:

Linda for introducing me to surf life,
Ramon, who inspires me to create my life the way i want it to be and to **Angie**, who as my surf coach and friend always encourages me to paddle forward in water but also in life. Seriously, without you the lavadora would be just another instagram-image. - Thank you!

Angie Ringleb
Surfcoach NOMB Surf
www.nombsurf.com

Mirjam Loosli
Graphic Artist Rambling Visuals
www.ramblingvisuals.com

Rainbow
Surferdog NOMB Surf
www.nombsurf.com

Annette Wahle
Ambassador children's rights
instagram / senatorin_w

Emilio de Armas
Surfcoach It´s On Surfcoaching
www.surfcoaching-tenerife.com

Josh Filgueiras
Surfcoach Grove Surfclub
www.waipiasurfschool.es

Lee Wood
Surfcoach Narosa Life
www.narosalife.com

Linda Schenker
SEO Master Texterbau
www.texterbau.ch

Melina Pérez Noriega
Nurse & Surfcoach
instagram / zoe_noriega

Paul Cardwell Hounam
Surfcoach Lawaflow Lanzarote
www.lavaflowsurf.com

Rahel Klein
Journalist | Presenter
www.rahel-klein.com

Ramon Álvarez Otero
Surfcoach Grove Surfclub
www.waipiasurfschool.

EPIC WAVES FAMILY PRESENTS

¡Hola, Ola!

AN ILLUSTRATED GUIDE TO THE SPANISH SURF LINGO

A BOOK BY ANGIE RINGLEB & MIRJAM LOOSLI

ISBN: 9783755771203

Impressum

Bibliografische Information der Deutschen Nationalbibliothek: Die Deutsche Nationalbibliothek verzeichnet diese Publikation in der Deutschen Nationalbibliografie; detaillierte bibliografische Daten sind im Internet über dnb.dnb.de abrufbar.

Produced and published by: BoD – Books on Demand, Norderstedt